i

This book will give the reader some insights into the Korean Conflict through the eyes of a farm boy as he served the U.S. Army in Kentucky and Virginia. Many of the details are captured from the diary I kept, and the letters saved by my wife, providing a day-to-day snapshot of my experience.

Published By

Evansville, Indiana
www.cordonpublications.com
cora.seaman@hotmail.com
(812) 455-9260

First printing: September 2021
ISBN: 978-1-937912-62-8

LENNY'S

Korean Conflict Days

Leonard C. Meyer

2021

CREDITS

I thank God and acknowledge that He
provided me with the wisdom and foresight
to have my letters saved to provide
details for this document.

I also thank the following individuals for their
efforts in the development of this book:

Jean Meyer (deceased wife)
for saving most of the letters.

Karen Meyer (daughter) for transcribing and
preserving the letters (a monumental project).

Daryl Emowrey (grandson) for his computer
technology (beyond me).

Shea Emowrey (granddaughter-in-law) for
designing the book cover.

Jean Mullins (neighbor) for helping me
over my "writer's block."

FORWARD

Leonard Clarence Meyer was born on his father's farm, five miles North and 1½ miles East of Humboldt, South Dakota on March 9, 1932. That happened to be Cecil Meyer's 26th birthday, Leonard's Mother. He was named Leonard so he would not have a nickname. That worked for most of his life.

He had one sibling, Wanda, born the next year. When Leonard was six and ready to start the First grade in school, he would not go without his sister. Since his dad, Walter Meyer, was on the School Board it was arranged and they went through all twelve grades together.

When they were Freshmen in High School, their Dad was very ill and, after two trips to the Mayo Clinic, it was determined that he would never be strong enough to farm again. He found other agricultural related employment and Leonard became the full time farmer, using horses and later a Model B John Deere tractor.

After graduating from Humboldt High School in 1950, the Korean Conflict began. It was not declared a "War" until many years later. It became obvious that all males received draft notices as soon as they were 20 years of age.

This book will give the reader some insights to that "conflict" through the eyes of a farm boy as he served the U.S. Army in Kentucky and Virginia.

CHAPTER 1

Fort Sheridan, Illinois

I was drafted into the Army and received my notice in March to report in Sioux Falls, South Dakota on April 15, 1952. Shortly before that date, Dad asked me if I really wanted to go because, as a farmer, I could have avoided the draft. (I had been doing most of the farming since 1946, as Dad was not physically able to do it.) I said, "Yes." I felt it was my duty to my country. Nothing more was said about that. Dad rented the farm to a neighbor while I was gone, with the provision that it would be mine to farm when I came back.

Dad took me to Sioux Falls on April 15. The recruiting office (where I reported) was near the train depot. Dad stayed around for a while. After I was "sworn in," Dad and I had lunch together in a nearby tavern. Then he went home and I joined the other draftees/recruits.

That evening, we boarded a train for Chicago. Several fellows played cards all night, I tried to sleep. The next day, in Chicago, we went by bus to Fort Sheridan, Illinois. There we were issued clothes and a duffel bag, also got our haircut and shots.

One evening an older Sergeant showed us how

to pack our duffel bag with a minimum of wrinkling of the clothes – Boots on the bottom and dress shoes on top. Needless to say, my clothes were soon too large for me. I weighed 220 pounds when I left home and was soon down to 190 pounds.

On the last night there, the Lutheran Chaplain offered Communion to anyone interested. Two of us went to his office. The other recruit was from Hartford, South Dakota and was a Missouri Synod Lutheran and I was an American Lutheran.

We went from there to Camp Breckinridge, Kentucky by bus.

CHAPTER 2

Basic Training at Camp Breckinridge, Kentucky – 1952

We took a "battery" of tests early on, whether at Fort Sheridan, or Camp Breckinridge I don't remember. Anyway, I apparently had a high score (140) on the Officer Candidate test and the Commandant at Breckinridge sent a letter to my Mother suggesting that I sign up for Officer Candidate School. I did sign up for that school as I wanted to learn as much as I could and stay out of Korea as long as possible. While processing out in April 1954, the fellow reviewing my paperwork said that he had reviewed thousands and had only seen one higher score (155) on that test and that fellow had a Master's Degree from college.

HEADQUARTER:
101 st AIRBORNE DIVISION AND CAMP BRECKINRIDGE
CAMP BRECKINRIDGE, KENTUCKY
OFFICE OF THE DIVISION COMMANDER

31 May 1952

Mrs. Walter A. Meyer
Humboldt, S. Dak.

Dear Mrs. Meyer:

    I am pleased to send you a picture of your son
and to inform you that he has arrived at Camp Breckinridge,
Kentucky, for training with the famed 101st Airborne Division.

    I am especially pleased to inform you that Army Tests
indicate he has the mental qualifications which will allow him
to apply for training as an Army Officer. I truly hope that
he proves to have the requisite physical capacity, educational
background, latent leadership ability and ambition to become
an officer. You may be assured that all his officers will
actively encourage him to qualify and compete for Army Officer
Candidate School training while he is at Camp Breckinridge.
Your personal encouragement to this objective will be of immense
value.

    You are welcome to visit him while he is here but it will
be necessary for you to obtain reservations in advance for lodg-
ing, either in one of the surrounding communities or in one of
the Guest Houses maintained at Camp Breckinridge. Because of
the limited number of rooms available, it will be necessary that
your application for reservations reach us at least seven days
prior to your proposed visit and should be addressed to:

        The Family Information Center
        Camp Breckinridge, Kentucky.

    The enclosed picture is suitable for reproduction in your
local newspaper.

    With kindest personal regards, I am

        Sincerely yours,

        RAY E. PORTER
        Major General, USA
        Commanding

No one told me that I would have to pay for some of my clothes and that I would have to send my "civies" home. Those costs were deducted from my first paycheck.

Learning to march in formation was interesting. The Drill Sergeant kept saying "Stretch 'em out." Well I did, and got called out of formation and he said, "You are used to walking on corn rows." I agreed and then he said "Shorten your stride. The corn rows are 36-inches apart and the stride in formation is only 30-inches. These city boys need to stretch out to that length." I didn't have any more problems after that.

A Colonel gave us a talk one day and explained how to conserve toilet paper. Use only one square at a time. Fold it into a triangle and then again until you have a small triangle. Then tear off the point and put it in your pocket for later. Put your finger through the hole in the center of the square and wipe carefully. Then fold the square back over your finger and wipe it clean. Then use the corner you tore off to clean under your fingernail.

He also asked us whether we had egg shells for breakfast. No one admitted it and then he told us we must not have eaten there as the scrambled eggs always have some shells in them.

When we were in class, we were told to swing out our elbows while seated to wake up those sitting next to us. The Instructor would call out: "Fly Boy!" when we were to do that.

I volunteered for everything, at first, as it was usually something to do outside; paint, rake the yard, etc. After a few days of that, I was told to stay in formation and go to class.

One evening we went out in the country and sat around, without striking a match, or any other form of light. When it got quite dark, a staff person lit a match about a half mile away. WOW! We got the message about light traveling in the dark of night.

Someone at the USO gave "ballroom dance lessons." We were given the basic foot movements, across the floor and the next week the lesson was the same. Useless!

Once, while on KP in Breckinridge, a soldier loaded potatoes into the new potato peeler (much like a washing machine) without any instructions and tumbled them until they were very small potatoes. Most of the potatoes went down the drain. They were only supposed to be tumbled until the skins were off. (I understand a similar process is used today to make small carrots.)

Another time, I observed some boxes (cases) of rabbit meat that was passed off as chicken. Interestingly, I could not tell the difference after the meat was cooked.

Besides the classroom and marching routines, we were given a variety of other instructions. One was a demonstration of using a tank to pick up a wounded soldier on the battlefield. The "wounded" person laid still in a "straight line" position and the tank drove over him. There is a "door" in the bottom of the tank and the tank stops over the individual, who is then raised into the tank. This is not an easy thing to do, as the tank driver cannot see the individual on the ground and must be directed by another crew member.

Another point to remember was that we, Americans, are prone to "fix" things that don't "look right." For example, when checking a building for enemy personnel, don't stop to straighten a crooked picture on the wall as it may be booby trapped.

There was a dam (reservoir), named Des Islet, on the post with a floating platform in the middle of it and a sandy beach on one side. A place to cool off on the weekends. Sometimes there were some girls there, usually just soldiers. I tried swimming, with no success. There was a fellow from Louisiana who liked to swim up behind someone underwater, and come up, clap his hands together, and say: "Gator gotcha!"

Refreshment shack on beach
at Des Islet lake.

The second in command, after the Platoon
Sergeant, was a Corporal from Scotland. He had
a room at the end of the barracks. At night, he
would often play the "pipes," without the bag. It
was a very soft sound which didn't disturb anyone

and I enjoyed it.

I was in 16 weeks, heavy weapons, Basic. We learned how to set up and fire the 5.2 inch mortar. We went on several hikes in the hot Kentucky summer and a week's bivouac. Our assigned "shelter" was a shallow spot covered with sticks and dirt with a low opening at the head end. Fairly comfortable, for sleeping on the ground. A small lizard seemed to like it as well. We were taught how to "clean up." Brush teeth first and wash socks last, using the same water (a helmet full). Got water from a 36-gallon Lister bag, disinfected with Chlorine tablets. It was quite hot in Kentucky that summer. When we took a break from marching/hiking, we were issued salt tablets to induce us to drink more water.

With a class A pass (earned after a certain number of weeks in Basic) one could go up to 200 miles "off post" on a weekend. Some of us went to Chicago (a bit over 200 miles) and I went on to Zion, Illinois to visit with Ted Barenklau, my dad's cousin. We went to Wisconsin on Sunday to get some beer. Ted invited a neighbor girl, Jean Radke, over Sunday afternoon. It was a pleasant visit. I went back to Chicago and joined the other fellows for our return to Camp Breckinridge. We made the whole trip without incident.

One night, while on bivouac, a fellow had

contacted his cousin who was stationed at Fort Campbell, Kentucky to come over and take some of us to a nearby town, Morganfield, Kentucky to see a drive-in movie. All went well for our group. We did not go to the concession stand. Some other fellows went to the same movie and to the concession stand and got picked up by the MPs. They were returned in the morning. We kept still.

In the 15th week we went through the Infiltration Course. We had to crawl through an area under strands of barbed wire, with machine guns firing overhead. For our safety, the machine guns were locked in position to fire only straight ahead, about three feet above the barbed wire. So, as long as we kept down, we wouldn't get shot. Still scary at night when tracer bullets were used. We were scheduled to go through the course twice during the daytime and once at night. Well, since I never learned to crawl when I was a youngster (still can't), I had to pull myself through with my elbows. There was a time limit for completing the course. After the time was up, the guns were turned off and those of us still out there were told to stand up and walk out. I was not alone. Some fellows simply "froze up" and couldn't move. After my first attempt, I went to the Medic and got bandages on my elbows as I had scraped off some skin. He kept me there while the second "crawl" was conducted. He said: "You can go again tonight."

Of course, we were taught the usual basics of Army life: all hand held weapons, the bayonet, hand to hand combat, physical exercises, marching, proper uniforms, polish shoes, boots and belt buckles, make up the bed, organize the wall and foot locker. The reader can ask any soldier for details about these.

With Basic over, several of us were "free" to come and go as we pleased, while waiting for Leadership School (another eight weeks). That will be another Chapter.

CHAPTER 3

Leadership School

Before this 8 week school could start, we had to wait for recruits from Fort Leonard Wood, Missouri. With a Class A pass, we were rather "free to roam" on and off post. When the new fellows arrived, we were all restricted to the post for two weeks (to give the new fellows time to get adjusted to the Post). Well, three of us "old timers" were a bit cocky and drove (one fellow had a car there) into Morganfield, Kentucky for gas and ice cream. No problem, until we went into the ice cream store. Our Executive Officer was seated there with a buddy of his, in civilian clothes, and we didn't recognize him until he had spotted us. He asked us what we were doing in town. We explained that we had come to town for gas and decided to stop for some ice cream before going back to camp. He then told us to report to the CO the next morning. We expected the worst when we did that.

The CO understood and contacted the Mess Sergeant and asked him if he could find some "detail" to keep us occupied every night for the next week (the second "restricted" week). He said he could and we were then directed to report to him every night for a week at 7 PM for a two-hour detail. Well, that was interesting, our "detail" was to "straighten up" the storeroom. (The cooks just never got around to doing it.) Condiments were received on a regular basis, regardless of the usage rate. Not a problem, we had the storeroom "ship shape" in about an hour. Then we sat around in it and stayed off the floor, out of the way of "special details" and others. When a new shipment of condiments came in, we stocked it with those already there. Great assignment.

Till J.N. Peters and Leonard Meyer at parade rest

While at Leadership School, the students wore blue armbands on their left arms. They appear black in the photo.

Early, during Leadership Training, we would march before breakfast, starting at "Double Time" and then dropping back to "Quick Time" (regular pace). One morning a seventeen-year old, from Detroit, in front of me was out of step and I hit his foot. Over his shoulder he said, "Do that again and I will hit you." By that time, we had taken another step so he hit me in my mouth. He broke off a front tooth. By then, he was back in step. As a result, he broke his "special" ring. When we got back, I reported to the Orderly room and was sent to Sick Bay, where a Dentist removed the rest of that tooth and made an impression for a single tooth partial. I used that partial until the Fall of 1953 when I got a bridge put in. (In Fort Belvoir, Virginia) Back in the Orderly room, the First Sergeant told me that whatever happened over the hill (behind the barracks) would be between the recruit and me. Since I have never been a "fighter" and the punk was "street smart," I let it go. After all, fighting would not bring back the tooth and might "cost" me more. He pestered me every night for a while. When we finished Leadership School, he had changed (The Lord handled it.) We parted as friends.

About this time, Herman Hotchkiss, a neighbor and High School classmate from Humboldt, South Dakota who was stationed at Fort Knox, Kentucky came over for his last weekend in Kentucky.

Leonard Meyer and Herman Hotchkiss

We three, Herman, Till J.N. Peters (a buddy in Leadership School) and I went into town on that Sunday. No recollection about how we got there. We went to the soda fountain to check out the girls and got "picked up" by an older fellow who offered to take us to Kentucky Lake and back. Since it was a nice day and there was a "beach" there, we decided to go with him. We didn't really plan on swimming, just looking at the girls. When we got there, he put on his trunks and started for the water. The concrete ramp was covered with moss. He slipped and split his head a little bit. The Lifeguard patched him up. So much for that! We ended up at his home on the north side of whatever town that was. He had a rock collection and other things. It began to get late and we were concerned about getting back to Post. We came to the conclusion that he had not intended to take us back to where he found us. We finally decided to get out of there, before we got ourselves into real trouble. We managed to get out to the highway and started "hitch-hiking." Fortunately, a Greyhound bus came by bound for Fort Knox. We flagged it down. Herman had his ticket from Camp Breckinridge to Fort Knox and the driver had pity on us and let Till and me ride to the main gate at Camp Breckinridge. The driver let us off at the main gate to Camp Breckinridge. We had to walk about two miles back into the camp to the Leadership School barracks. Herman made it back to Fort Knox and on to South Dakota the next week. He had to leave his "ditty" bag (some called it an AWOL bag) at my barracks. The following weekend, Till and I took the Greyhound bus over to Fort Knox and after much wrangling with the station keeper, we took Herman's ditty bag and sent it on its way to South Dakota.

After Leadership School (Training), I had two weeks "orderly room" duty, since it was too early to go to my next assignment (Engineer Officer Candidate School) at Fort Belvoir, Virginia. My assignment was to keep the orderly room neat (orderly) during the day – put things away, mop the floor and handle mail call. Tough job!

Several times while in Camp Breckinridge, I would take the bus into Evansville, Indiana on Friday evening and return Sunday afternoon. While there, I would go to the Servicemen's Club, a former Fire Station in downtown Evansville. Since it had been the garage for fire trucks, there was a large room, which became a dance hall. There were a couple of pool tables on the second floor. Soldiers could get a cup of coffee and a piece of angel food cake free. At that time, I did not drink coffee and as I remember, we were limited to one piece of cake per visit. Iglehart Brothers Milling Company furnished the cakes (makers of Swansdown cake flour). All cakes were white angel food when received with an edge cut off one side, for testing purposes. If a fellow wanted it chocolate, chocolate syrup was poured on it. (Jean Cox, later my wife, never believed that as she was sure they actually got chocolate cake.) I often helped out behind the counter and served many pieces, both ways.

Being a recruit (Private), I had very little money to spend after the bus ticket to/from Evansville.

I learned that I could stay at the YMCA for $1 a night. This was about a block from the Servicemen's Club. One Saturday, I was out of money and went into the YMCA by the back door. (You see I had learned how to avoid the "front desk.") After a good night's sleep, I awoke to be the only one left in the barracks. There on the footlocker at the foot of my bed, were some bills - a few ones and a five and maybe a ten. I figured someone left it there for me, so I used them, and thanked the LORD! I left the usual rate for the use of the bed and went on my way.

The latter part of October, I was still there and still waiting for papers to go to Fort Belvoir. The Servicemen's Club had an early Halloween Dance and I hoped to dance with a certain girl. Well, that was not to be. She was very popular and I didn't have a chance. Looking around, I found a girl that wasn't dancing and figured that she was for me. SHE WAS! We made a date for a "GI" picnic the next week and the fellow who had a car also made a date (as did another couple - six total) and we took them to Mesker Park for a "GI" picnic (leftovers from C rations and 5-in-1 rations) crackers, preserves, candy, canned fruit, canned meat, chocolate bars and Tootsie Rolls. All seemed to have a good time.

For my next date with Jean Cox, I bought a pair of "dressy" trousers, as I had been wearing blue jeans when I was off post. Jean didn't like that as she had always told the girls, she would never date a fellow in blue jeans and here she was doing that. We went to the Mesker Park Zoo, where they had a monkey island that was interesting to watch. The island was surrounded by a moat so the monkeys couldn't get off. There was a tree on it for them to swing. It was a warm October Sunday afternoon and she took her jacket off and I carried it. She kept offering to take it back and I finally had to tell her that the zipper on my new trousers had stuck down when I went to the rest room. I was using it to cover the gap.

One Friday afternoon in October we were loaded on a bus and taken to Lynnville, Indiana. We were there to look for a local fellow who was missing. He had gone out looking for deer trails, preparing for hunting season. His car was parked just off the road in an old driveway. The area was covered with deep ditches, some with water in them, left after the coal had been removed. We "fanned out" and looked over a small area that evening. Then we were fed and told that we would cover a large area on Saturday. It was hot and humid (no breeze). Some fellows slept in the bus. I slept on the ground between some cornrows.

After breakfast, we were given maps to use for recording where we had been and to record open wells, and other places one could fall into. There were many abandoned homesteads in the area where the landowners had sold their land to the coal company. We did not find him. However, we did not search a line of trees about two blocks away from where we started. We were not told why we didn't search there. We were taken back to Camp and the fellows who didn't go with us were then free to go on leave. Well, we could go on leave too, but we were tired and filthy.

The next day, Sunday, two local couples, went looking for deer trails and found the fellow's body in that line of trees.

That's enough about that Camp. I took the train from Evansville, Indiana to Sioux Falls, South Dakota for a short leave before reporting to Fort Belvoir, Virginia for The Engineers Officer Candidate School (TEOCS) in November '52.

On my train ride from Evansville, Indiana to

Sioux Falls, South Dakota I had failed to make a reservation and had to get one from the conductor. Slept a couple of hours on the way to Chicago.

On the train west out of Chicago, I met a WAVE. She is from Iowa and is stationed in Alexandria, Virginia. She has been there two and a half years and is 23 years old. I got her address in Virginia.

While home, I went with some neighbor fellows to the Arkota Ballroom in Sioux Falls, South Dakota for a "Sadie Hawkins" Dance. The Arkota did not serve liquor, only soft drinks and coffee. Patrons were allowed to bring their own liquor to the Arkota. Well, I danced several times and didn't notice that the liquid in my 7up bottle didn't go down. I fell asleep almost as soon as I got in the car to go home. They woke me when we got to my home, at least forty minutes later. I slept well that night. Later, I was informed that the guys had been pouring some liquor in my 7up bottle every time I was dancing.

One Sunday I went to church with my folks and sister, Wanda, after which we went to Canistota to see my Grandma Meyer. We took along a roast for dinner. After dinner we went out in the country to visit with Dad's second cousin and family. They had two boys, about eighteen and fourteen. The eighteen-year old had gone goose hunting. In the evening, I picked up an old buddy of mine and we went to Montrose to a small roller rink. I failed to take my shoe skates and wore blisters on my ankles.

While there, I helped my Dad "seal" corn. I took the samples out of the cribs while he did the paperwork. I drove between farms. Shot a pheasant with my .22 rifle. Out of season and with an illegal weapon.

A few days later, we (Dad, Mom and sister, Wanda) went to Cottonwood and Philip in western South Dakota to visit my Grandma Palmer and other relatives out there. We celebrated an early Thanksgiving at Dad's Aunt Annie O'Dea's place. They had two big turkeys as they have a large family and there were thirty-eight people there. They seem closer than cousins, one girl is my age. Dad met Mom when she was working for Annie several years ago. An older couple (Albert and Emma Bork) came out from Humboldt to "watch" the farm while we were gone. They had known Dad since he was little.

Another evening, we went to Canistota for a Thanksgiving dinner with all of Dad's relatives at Theis Whitrock's place, where Grandma Meyer worked. (Dad's twin brothers Elmer and Wilmer and their families and those cousins who lived near Canistota.) The next day, I did some Christmas shopping in Sioux Falls and got my train ticket to

D.C. – $45.08, pretty cheap!

My mother made corsages from the small pheasant feathers around the rooster's neck. I took one for Jean and a few for some of the girls at the Servicemen's Center in Evansville. (In my letters to Jean, I kept saying that I wished she were here.)

Before I left home, we had family Thanksgiving Dinner at our home place. All my relations on Dad's side were there, including my Grandma Meyer and the fellow she works for, plus Dad's twin brothers and their families. Also, there was the cousin from Canistota, his family and his brother.

CHAPTER 4

TEOCS, Fort Belvoir, Virginia

When I got to D.C., I did some sightseeing. (I had been there in February of 1951.) I rode the elevator to the top of the Washington Monument and walked down the 800+ steps. Walked along the Reflection Pool to the Lincoln Memorial. Looked it over thoroughly.

Then back to the Soldiers, Sailors, Marines and Airman's Club at 1015 L Street NW, about a block from the White House, where I stayed overnight. I went out to Fort Belvoir the next day by bus that was the end of Leadership School and furlough.

First thing Saturday morning at TEOCS, we had two inspections. One was a "standby" (standby your bunk and foot locker); the other was rifle. I didn't do the worst, about average. Then we had to write our autobiography. My bunkmate, "Mike" Magyar (pronounced major) is from Connecticut, and seems to be a swell guy. The food here is excellent, served family-style. We will get C rations on Friday, just like in Breckinridge.

We'd get up at 5:45 AM, and at 5:55 AM we are in formation for Reveille. We must be in bed at 10:15 PM. Lights are out, no sounds afterward.

Mattress and blankets are folded up during the day and can't be unfolded until after 9:15 PM.

First Sunday evening we had a "bull session" to get the "poop" on the school and company regulations. School started the next day and then all upperclassmen could correct us. We had a sample today. It will be rough. This is the next thing to West Point. There were three pages of stuff to memorize in the first two weeks.

As Officer Candidates, we could not go to the Enlisted Men's Service Clubs, or to the Officer Clubs. There was a Candidate Club in the basement of the barracks building to which we could go after our 7th week. After our 4th week, if we didn't have over 6 gigs, we could go out on post from Saturday noon until 10 PM and again on Sunday.

What a contrast between the wooden barracks in Camp Breckenridge and the two-story brick barracks here, with a basement. Still double deck metal bunks and metal lockers.

As Plebes, all upperclassmen can correct us. We had two inspections before starting classes. One was a "standby" (standing by your bunk and foot locker); the other was a rifle inspection. We had to write an autobiography and read a book over the weekend before the first class.

1 December - The first day of school. I liked it very much. Just like college they say only more condensed. Company A, won a parade today. First time in the history of TEOCS that a company with a Plebe class won a parade. But we fouled up immediately as we left barracks tonight with our clothes, etc., scattered all over. The Senior Officer of the Day (a Senior candidate) came through. He didn't like what he saw, so now as they say here we've "had it."

Also, the Company will have late lights tonight (11:00), more work.

Had to learn "Plebe Knowledge" including the first and last verses of the Star Spangled Banner.

One Saturday morning we had a battalion inspection (by a Lieutenant Colonel). Then we went through the Confidence Course. Got my boots all muddy. Came in at 11:50 and at noon we were in the dining hall. Changed clothes, of course, as we eat in Class A on weekends. At 12:45 PM we, the guards, fell out for a preliminary inspection. For some unexplainable reason, I put on the same dirty boots. I was "kicked off " of the guard. The first time in the history of OCS here at Fort Belvoir and it had to be me. My upper bunkmate took my place and I filled in for him at KP the next day (Sunday).

I don't know what will happen to me. I might have to appear before some Board or other. I'm pretty sure that I am on probation for that.

I went to sleep in class again this morning. I'll have to write a letter of explanation for sleeping. I had to meet with a Junior that evening @ 9:45 PM and know all of my Plebe Knowledge.

Three weeks of classes and then about ten days off for Christmas and New Year's. I rode to

Waterloo, Iowa with a classmate. Then I took the train to Sioux Falls, South Dakota. I was "home for Christmas."

I went by train from Sioux Falls to Evansville, Indiana for New Year's with Jean and her folks, Ronald and Gladys Cox. I had met them while I was at Camp Breckinridge. Very accommodating folks. On New Year's Day, I walked around the corner to St. Mark's Lutheran church about 10 AM for their service. (This was not unusual, at the time, for churches to have services on New Year's Day.) On the way back, I found a man's wedding ring on the sidewalk. I took it to the front door of that house and asked if someone there had lost it. I had to knock several times to get someone to answer the door. An elderly fellow, with a slurred voice asked: "What do you want?" I told him about finding the ring in front of his house and asked if it might belong to someone there. He responded: "Nah!" And shut the door. Since it fit, I thought I might as well keep it. The only info carved inside it was, "14 carat art carved." I left it with Jean in case someone advertised for it.

The night I was planning to catch a bus from Evansville to Indianapolis, Indiana I had an appendicitis attack and was in too much pain to move. The pain subsided in time for me to catch a later bus and still get to Indianapolis by noon. (The time I had planned to meet my ride back to Fort Belvoir.) One of the other TEOCS classmates had to stop by and say good-bye to a girl friend in a small town between Indianapolis and Richmond. That delayed us a bit, but we still got to DC the next morning. We went to a barbershop for a real shave and haircut before reporting in at Fort Belvoir. Serious training for several weeks.

One week, I operated a Caterpillar grader, a Bucyrus Erie 15B shovel and a Caterpillar Diesel tractor. Now I am studying our General Orders. I had guard duty one evening in a gentle snow. I went to the dispensary one morning and they gave me some red stuff in a bottle. They suggested taking one teaspoon full after each meal. Maybe only sugar water, as it tasted sweet. I did have slight pain while doing PT. Otherwise my side seemed better.

We built floating bridges and rafts this week and had a familiarization course on Surveying.

We built part of a big (50 ton capacity) floating bridge one afternoon. We drove the big crane, on a truck, out on the bridge. It didn't sink. One thing about stuff like that is that we never had to take it down.

Our class had guard duty one night this week. Then we had to scrape helmet liners to get them in shape for the Inaugural Parade. I was placed on

Probation because I was deficient in all phases. Academic, 1 point below passing; Conduct just below passing; PT 20 some points below passing; Military Aptitude down how far I didn't know. I had to go to the Tactical Officer again. Although I thought this was the end, he "chewed" me quite a bit and he actually made me feel a little better. I will have to work hard to stay with the class.

20 January 1953 - *Inauguration Day*. Several TEOCS soldiers stood guard along Pennsylvania Avenue, without weapons. It was a cold, windy day. The regular Army troops across the Avenue were armed with M-1 rifles. They had to get a spectator out of a tree. The parade lasted from 1:45 PM till 6:35 PM. I stood out there until 5 PM and then I had to a take a short break. I was hoping to see the South Dakota float. However, I had to go to the restroom and that was about two blocks away, same building where we had our lunch. When I got back, the South Dakota float was almost out of sight. Oh well, I did see Truman and Eisenhower in the morning when Truman was still the President and again in the afternoon when "Ike" was President. So, I saw two Presidents on the same day, when they were each President. A long tiring day! I did see several other floats including Indiana, Kentucky, Illinois, Iowa, Texas, Minnesota and Nebraska.

One afternoon we had clothing formations,

from class D to A in eight minutes. A to C in five minutes. C to D and back to B for the fellows that made it to formation in correct uniform. The rest had full field and back to class B. That was really some racing, as we had to hang everything up neatly and button it. I was assistant class leader at this point in time. That is the same as Platoon Sergeant. It is next to the highest job you can get as a Plebe.

28 January - I was informed that I had to write a letter of explanation for missing English on Saturday, January 17. I was working tours that day and hence impossible to get to class. But, I must explain. They are not hard to write, just take time and I don't have a sample to go by.

One morning one of the boys found a frog. We brought it in and put it under one of the Junior's plate this noon. He happened to be my table Commandant. He raised up his plate and the frog didn't move. He told me to take it out. I reached for it and away it went onto another Juniors' silverware. Then another Junior caught it and handed it to me. Some fun. He did take it as a joke for a wonder.

We will have our class party at the Raleigh Hotel in DC. It will cost $10.50 per couple and $7.50 stag. I wrote to the Wave asking her to go with me. She didn't answer, so I am going with one of the girls associated with the Candidate Club. High-class stuff. Ha! Ha! They are from the Embassies.

I did not have to go before the 6th week Board. There were nine observation reports on me. All unsatisfactory. I failed one subject, but my average was above passing so that was OK. I am still on probation. I was warned that unless my Military Aptitude improves, I would have to go before the 12th week Board.

One night several Plebes dressed in fatigues, soft cap and work gloves went into the Junior's squad room and set up a gin pole for one of the Juniors. Another day we went way out into the country and looked at a couple of bridges. We measured them and figured the amount of explosives required to blow them up and where to place the charges.

I don't know the Morse Code but I have the "Engineer's Bible," his FM (Field Manual) 5-34. It is loaded with all kinds of formulas, etc: including Morse Code, Signal Flag code, panel code. Lots of stuff.

We had regular guard duty and also as a penalty for demerits (anything that wasn't done to the satisfaction of whoever inspected you, or your equipment was given a demerit.) One of the buildings we guarded was classified and we were not told what went on inside, only that there was a locked room at one end of it on the second floor. The person on guard sat at the head of the stairs, facing the front door at the bottom of the stairs. This was the only place where the guard was allowed to sit down. All other "posts" were walking "posts" around certain buildings.

Demolitions were demonstrated, thankfully, as I didn't want to get too close to the explosives. Rope and Rigging was taught by demonstration and hands-on. We had to "teach" some classes, such as bayonet. We laid out an anti-tank mine field, using mines with fuses set, but no explosive. We changed sides and dug them up. Some fellows "blew" themselves up, as they didn't use the correct procedure. I got all the safeties in and the mines out and disarmed OK. I have more respect for mines now and am not afraid of them anymore.

All weapons used by the Infantry and Engineers were reviewed and fired on the firing range. I qualified with the M-1 Rifle, carbine, .45 caliber sub machine gun, .45 caliber pistol, and .30 caliber machine gun. We actually had learned to use these while in Basic Training and this was a review for some of us. We had to disassemble and reassemble most of them.

Military Sanitation, Tactics, Staff Organizing and Procedures were among the subjects taught.

Some Saturday nights a bus load of girls from an embassy would come to the basement of our barracks for an evening of dancing/visiting. These primarily were from European Embassies. No alcohol allowed, yet sometimes the punch bowl was spiked.

One lesson was about etiquette at official dinners. We were issued white gloves for the occasion and then instructed in how to eat properly. Well, the gloves were placed on your belt, just so. Then when getting soup from your soup bowl, you were to dip the spoon into the bowl in front of you and then move it across the bowl to get it full. Then lift it straight up and bring it to your mouth, thereby describing a square meal.

(I'm still not too sure that wasn't in jest.) However, it did keep you from sloshing the soup onto yourself.

English Correspondence course was near the end of the Plebe stage. I had to read the Officer Candidate Regulations again and sign a certificate to the effect. I was getting rather "mushy" in my letters to Jean.

I went to a U.S.O. dance in DC at the Jewish Community Center. There was a big dance floor, about the size of the one at the Servicemen's Club #1 in Breckinridge. I danced with girls from Maine, Rhode Island, Maryland, DC, North Carolina and Nebraska, WAVEs and WAFs. One works in the Justice Department. I had a lot of fun. It sounds like I really got around doesn't it? Well, they had a good mixer and a grand march.

10 February - I received my first satisfactory observation report and another that wasn't too bad. The first one was for PT. The first instructor didn't know his exercises, so I gave seven exercises, eight repetitions of each plus the two repetitions of each for demonstration purposes. Boy, am I tired, but happy. So are the Tactical Officers. They like to see one progress.

I have started Fixed Bridges, a rough course. Statistics show that every platoon leader (2nd Lieutenant) in an Engineer Combat Construction Co. spends one day out of every six on bridging (building, repairing, maintaining, or blowing). I got through the job of Class Leader all right, and became Assistant Charge of Quarters. Also, I gave a talk on the Chinese Situation, not a lecture, just a Conference.

I went to the dance at the Candidate Club Saturday night. I had fun; I danced two dances and watched TV the rest of the evening. One dance was the Mexican Hat Dance. The band was lousy. They played funeral marches. I had signed for a date. She didn't come. There was a girl without a date, so I took her. I always get a good-looking girl. The other fellows who asked for dates didn't get such good looking ones.

We got a new member in our class last Saturday. He was set back from class 48B (We are class 49A).

He had been on five-day Emergency Leave, which caused the set back. One can't miss that much instruction here and still get by.

Our Company is sponsoring the Saturday night party and dance on the 7th of March at the O/C (Officer Candidate) club. "Bingo" is planned for the first hour. I will celebrate my 21st birthday, then, as I will be too busy on Monday (the 9th). As Juniors, we are authorized to wear brass off post; the U.S. with red disks under them. They really look sharp. When we become Seniors, we will wear the Castles with red disks under them. I asked Jean to make a box of cookies for my Birthday. (She had sent boxes of cookies several times while I was here. Some other folks had sent cookies also.)

21 February - We passed inspection this morning. Everyone looked good and we all had clean rifles. I had a four hour detail this afternoon, took the wax off the upper hall and Class 49A's Tactical Office and the T I and E room.

Right after dinner, we moved out to the porch or hall, whichever one would call it. It has a concrete floor and runs the length of the building on one side. It is about twelve-feet wide. That means a lot less area to clean and a little more crowded. We moved to make room for the new Plebes. We, Juniors, are down to twenty-three now. There is a dance at the O/C Club tonight, French girls. I hear about half of them are good looking. I shined my boots tonight.

I went to church the next morning and then was restricted until 7 PM, after that I had Guard Mount and I was Corporal of the Guard. Monday was a Holiday (Washington's Birthday). We were in a parade in Alexandria. Last Friday there was a rough football game. One fellow sprained his right hand and another went to the hospital with a possible brain concussion. He was expected back next week. Spring is coming, the jonquils are coming up. We were issued sweaters last week.

Next week we study pile driving, cement mixing (to make concrete) and Engineer Reconnaissance. My academic scores are on the upgrade. We will finish Fixed Bridges next week then we will have the final in Soils after that. It is supposed to be the roughest course here.

March 7 - I had to help decorate the O/C Club for the Company party. I signed for a date. I asked for the homeliest one. Wonder if I will get her. Had a date with a girl that I met at the O/C Club a couple of weeks ago. Her mother is visiting from West Virginia. We went to Arlington Cemetery and around Lee's Mansion. I am in charge of a Plebe detail tonight, the first time for me. Tomorrow, we become full-fledged Juniors at noon and the Plebes become part of the Company.

The O/C Club party went well. I had a lot of fun. There was a graduate nurse from New York who has been in DC for five weeks. We celebrated St. Patrick's Day with Green and Orange punch.

I got by the 12th Board by the skin of my teeth according to Lieutenant Shaeffer. He said the skin would have to be a lot thicker for the 18th week Board because then all doubt is considered in favor of the school. At the 6th and 12th Boards, doubt is considered in favor of the student. My average score is over 80 now, so if I get my Military Aptitude and PT up a bit, I should graduate.

We finished Command and Staff Procedure and Signal Communications is next. Bivouac was in the middle of March. It was cold out there and I only got two hours of sleep. After that, we turned in our bayonets, as we won't need them any more here. The classes get easier as we get closer to the end. We have been doing some "processing out as enlisted men" and signing up for our first assignment as an officer. I signed up for twenty-four months and Austria (where Herman Hotchkiss is stationed).

As Juniors, we now have only one hour of study hall each night. We are entitled to two evening passes, on post, each week. More free time, with more responsibility. We will be pulling Sergeant of the Guard, Jr. and Sr. Officer of the Guard, Jr. and Sr.

Officer of the Day.

Had our graduation photos taken with an officer's hat and bars on the shoulders.

Next week we will start ordering our uniforms. The uniforms will cost $250 and we get an allowance of $100. Such a deal! We will go to Fort McNair, in DC, to parade for General Van Fleet who is retiring. The cherry trees are in bloom.

This Weapons course is a review of Basic Training, covering it all in two weeks instead of ten, still boring.

March 25 - I had my "buddy" reports read to me. I have to improve posture and voice and learn to give the right impression. By that I mean the class is getting the wrong impression of my feelings concerning this school and constructive criticism. I like the school and appreciate the criticism, but have given some the impression that I don't. I found that all twenty-two men remarked on my good cooperation with the class. That fact impressed Lieutenant Shaeffer very much. Lieutenant Shaeffer told me if I didn't improve my Military Aptitude I would go before the 18th week Board. I intend to improve. I hope and pray that I do. I am on Probation again, but only for Military Aptitude this time. We are having our Khaki trousers altered now. We will start wearing them on May 2nd.

We paraded at Fort Lesley J. McNair, along with

the 3rd Infantry Division, in honor of General Van Fleet, who was retiring. There are several brick homes, with boat docks, along the canal out to the Potomac where retired Generals live.

I am supervising the Plebe study hall tonight. (Keeping the noise down and answering questions.) Soft job.

There is a WAC here who was at Camp Breckinridge, Kentucky. I haven't had a chance to talk to her yet. Her brother went to school with a buddy I used to have down there. I see her nearly every day as she walks past the TEOCS area towards Post headquarters.

This month I will get $1.25 per day for the fifteen days Christmas leave I had. This is an allowance for the meals I ate.

29 March - *Senior at last* We had a big track meet last Saturday afternoon. I cheered. Fox Company won the meet with eight Blues and three Red ribbons. We got a big trophy. I have been restricted all weekend (17 demerits). I was placed in charge of all details and work tours. All I had to do was supervise. At 4 PM, the Candidate Company Commander let me off. I went to the O/C Club and drank three beers. They sure tasted good. I went to church this morning. A member of my class was Baptized and Confirmed. I am going to church Thursday night (Maundy Thursday),

Holy Communion, or Lord's Supper. Easter Sunrise service is at 5:30 AM.

As Seniors, we are entitled to 2-week night Post passes per week. Only one hour of study hall and we can stay out all night Saturday nights. After study hall one night, we had to get our bookcases up from the basement. The Plebes had painted them the night before. Our class had Officers of the Guard that same night.

3 April - *Good Friday* - Fired 220 out of 250 on rifle range today. That is Expert. I am a Platoon Leader in the Company formation for tomorrow's inspection. I will have to inspect the rifles in my platoon. Mine will not be inspected. But I still have to clean it because fourteen clips, eight rounds each went through it yesterday and 100 some rounds went through today.

I received a letter from Herman. (Hotchkiss, my high school classmate, stationed in Austria.)

They have a 2nd Lieutenant who is leaving there in April so I may get a chance at it. Anyway I signed up for it as first choice (after graduation). If I get Austria, it would mean that I wouldn't have to go the other way. I would sooner fight in Europe than in Korea. Of course, I haven't got either yet. Besides that I haven't passed the 18th week Board yet.

Easter Sunday I went to Sunrise service at 5:30 and was Sergeant of the Guard at 12:45.

𝔈𝔞𝔰𝔱𝔢𝔯 𝔖𝔲𝔫𝔯𝔦𝔰𝔢
𝔖𝔢𝔯𝔳𝔦𝔠𝔢

5 April 1953   **0530 hours**

𝔉𝔬𝔯𝔱 𝔅𝔢𝔩𝔳𝔬𝔦𝔯, 𝔙𝔦𝔯𝔤𝔦𝔫𝔦𝔞

𝔐𝔞𝔧𝔬𝔯 𝔊𝔢𝔫𝔢𝔯𝔞𝔩 𝔖𝔱𝔞𝔫𝔩𝔢𝔶 𝔏. 𝔖𝔠𝔬𝔱𝔱, 𝔆𝔬𝔪𝔪𝔞𝔫𝔡𝔦𝔫𝔤

I wore a pistol, a real "Big Shot."

11 April - Our Company (Fox) has the O/C Club party. They are now putting liquor in the punch. We gave blood the same day. Our whole company volunteered to give a pint of blood each. It was a "big doings" with General Scott and Mrs. Charles E. Wilson here. (Her husband heads the Department of Defense.) They took a lot of pictures. I guess we set some kind of record for the most blood donated by one group at any one time. Some Air Force Base donated 300 pints awhile back. We donated 354 pints in six hours.

19 April - *30 more days.* We got back from our last bivouac this morning. We had been out since Wednesday. It was cold Thursday night, then beautiful Friday night and rained and was ice cold last night. While camped in the woods, about 3 AM a troop of other soldiers came storming through firing their guns and banging on metal, making a hellacious ruckus. By the time we got out of our tents, they were gone. Of course, in Korea the Chinese would have been shooting us.

In OCS, there were three classes, Plebe, Junior and Senior. One had to pass three "Boards" to advance to the next class. The first Board was at 6th weeks and the second at 12th-weeks. Any "doubt" was considered in favor of the student. The last Board was the 18th week Board and any "doubt" was in favor of the school. Military Law was the only subject left to take.

One significant factor in passing a Board was Military Aptitude. This was determined by the ranking each student gave to everyone in his class (including himself). One had to rank each student from best Military Aptitude to poorest. This was my weakest point, at both the 6th and 12th week Boards. On the 18th week Board, the Officers who determined the total score decided that my Military

Aptitude wasn't high enough. Interestingly, I had already had my "graduation picture" taken in an officer's uniform and had ordered new uniform clothes. Graduation ceremonies were to be held in the Essayons Playhouse where plays were performed. Essayons means "Let Us Try", which is the Corp of Engineers motto.

2 May - I did not pass the 18th week board on April 27 and was set back into a Junior class of 45 men with a few other fellows who were set back earlier. I will have three weeks as a Junior and should go back to Senior after that. I had all my notes from the classes I had been through. So, academically, the hardest part is the required two-hour study hall each weeknight for the next three weeks. I ordered my uniforms from the Quartermaster and will have them tailored there as well. Also, bought two sets of Gold brass. I WILL graduate on July 14.

I went to a Missouri Lutheran church in Alexandria and met a girl from Spencer, South Dakota (about 25 miles from home). She had been to our O/C Club party Saturday night. She is originally from Menno and knows some people I know in Spencer. She has been in Alexandria two years. The countryside is really beautiful, trees green, tulips and iris in bloom.

6 May - Rained yesterday and now it is hot

and humid. We had an hour of dismounted drill this morning and then double timed to class. Now my clothes are soaked with sweat. I'm looking forward to having Jean here on weekends. I asked Jean to bring the ring along, that I had found on the sidewalk, when she comes. I suggested to her that it might be better for her to take two weeks in July instead of a week in June, as originally planned. Then, perhaps, we could go to New York for a couple of days and check it out. I told her that my thoughts of her and me were running in one direction and it was not a life of friendship but one of a happy full life together.

On Armed Forces Day in May 1953, we went to DC to march in the parade. We "formed up" behind the Capitol while other troops got in position. We were put "At Ease," as long as we kept one foot in place and remained standing. The next unit over (regular troops) was allowed to relax, mingle around, even sit if they desired. Because of our limited activity, we had one fellow pass out. Eventually, we marched (paraded) down Constitution Avenue.

There was a new girl working in the O/C Club. Real sexy (a sweater girl). She sure draws the boys. The O/C Club has been in the red, as far as money goes for some time, this should change that. The boys won't admit that they go there just to look at her, but they do. She doesn't interest me.

I am ordering a new pair of boots and one pair of shoes on payday. Ordering 20 invitations and 100 name cards (like a high school or college graduation card). My name will be embossed on them as will Lieutenant.

I wrote to Jean that I was thinking of her more and more each day and a little more seriously each time. I felt as if I had known her from childhood on up. I guessed that I had really fallen in love with her and didn't mind it a bit.

One day we had a graded Practical Exercise. Since I had been through it before, I had the school solution. I was looking at it before the exercise. Someone (another set back fellow) said let me see that and I let him. It was passed around to 4 or 5 other fellows. I didn't think much about it at the time. But Friday night, the President of the Honor Committee asked me if I had let anyone see the solution and reminded me that it was an honor violation. He told me he would let me know more about it on Monday. I will probably have to go before the Honor Board. I could get kicked out for it, but the President said I shouldn't worry too much about it. In other words, I should be all right.

Now about the Honor Board. It is comprised of five senior members, one from the Senior class of each Company, and five Junior members from the next class in each Company. The last five don't vote. One of the first five is elected President. They are all elected from their respective classes. They meet and decide all honor cases. If one man votes that it is not an honor violation, the entire case is dropped, the records burned and everything forgotten. If unanimous, that it is an honor violation, it goes before Colonel Browning, OCS Commandant, and he will tell the Tactical Officers the man is relieved from duty and he will be dropped from the school immediately.

18 May - I am still lost, literally speaking. I expect to go before the Honor Board tomorrow night or Wednesday evening. One of my old classmates and former member of the Board gave me a couple of tips. He was the first one who sounded like I had a chance of beating the Board. It will take a couple of days to get the results of the meeting.

Right now we are studying the machine gun (boring class). I took the girl from Spencer, South Dakota to the party for class 49 (A and B) that night. She works at the Pentagon as a typist. She reminded me of my sister in size and shape. Seems like being at home to talk to her.

I wrote to Jean that the red roses were out all over the countryside and beautiful. Right now, it is impossible to make any plans for the future. I do have plans in my head about the future when the

Army is through with me.

19 May - Graduation exercises are over and I personally congratulated every member of my old class. My old Tactical Officer said: "You will make it this time." My date, from Spencer, wore a white formal and looked very nice. She had a swell time and I drank too much (the punch had been spiked) I thought about Jean that night and even called my date Jean. I explained that you were my girl back in Indiana. I still didn't know when the Honor Board was going to meet. My date told me to trust the Lord. Excellent advice.

20 May - I was supposed to go before the Honor Board tonight, but the case before mine drug out too long. So, I sat in the O/C Club and watched TV.

30 May - Still in OCS, Colonel Browning got the proceedings (or findings) last Thursday. So I should be relieved by Monday. I am going to really try to save some money when I leave here because Jean and I will need it. If I go to college, I will take up Civil Engineering. Qualified on the M-1 Rifle again. Also qualified on the Carbine this time. I plan to go to bed early tonight so I may not sleep in church tomorrow. That is a bad habit of mine to fall asleep when someone is lecturing or speaking.

2 June - I talked to Colonel Browning last night. He said he had no choice but to relieve me. He said he hoped I had learned from my mistake (as he called it). He said this is the only place where one doesn't get a second chance. It doesn't have any bearing on what kind of man one is. Just that one made a mistake. He gave me a choice, I could resign, or he would have me processed out of OCS.

When I got back to my unit, the Company Commander and the Executive Officer asked me what I would do about it. I said I would let him process me out. (This usually happened the next day.) Nothing happened on Tuesday. About midday Wednesday, I got a message to report to the Orderly Room. No one there seemed to have any idea why I was there. By that time, I decided to resign. I already had about fourteen months of my two year "enlistment" served and wasn't anxious to continue beyond the two years. So, I resigned and was transferred to Company D (The company for those awaiting Discharge).

I learned later that one would not be sent overseas with less than nine months to serve and I was down to ten. Effective the first of July, that Company name was changed to P, for Processing personnel on and off post. Several fellows in that company were dropouts from TEOCS and told me that the Supply Officer was looking for a Clerk-Typist. Since I had taken typing in High School, I mentioned that as I checked in. The Supply Officer asked me to copy some General Orders; these are primarily a jumble of letters and numbers. I copied a line or two and then he yanked the paper out of the typewriter and told them to assign me to that Company. From then on I was technically a Clerk-Typist.

CHAPTER 5

Clerk-Typist in the Mess Hall

There was a short period of time after I resigned before I was actually transferred to Company D, which became company P on July 1, 1953. I was transferred mid-June.

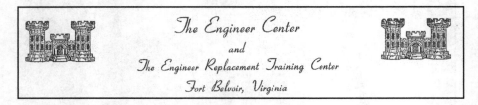

The Engineer Center
and
The Engineer Replacement Training Center
Fort Belvoir, Virginia

I started trips to the Dental Clinic to get a bridge put in to replace the one tooth partial that I got back in Breckinridge. As of June 20, I had three appointments scheduled in August. The X-ray technician, a WAC, knows a girl from Evansville, Indiana who is stationed here.

My first assignment in Company P was to "straighten out" the pass records in the Orderly Room. Everyone who had been through Basic Training was eligible for a pass. (There were a few restrictions). Since everyone coming on the Fort for training went through Company P, there were a lot of passes on file. Some were quite OLD as most fellows were usually there for a few days and their passes had not been removed from the file. Some fellows had been there for a week or more and had not been issued a pass. To add to the "confusion" new troops arrived almost daily (sometimes 500). I issued them passes, as permitted. It took me about three weeks to get the file straightened out and current.

I helped out at the Service Club to prepare for dances and shows. There were forty-five girls from DC one evening to put on a variety show and I operated the spotlight. (Made a hit with the ladies who came with the girls.) I also helped close up the Club. It gave me some exercise. I square danced with three girls from Ireland.

In the meantime, my folks cancelled their tentative trip to see me graduate from OCS in July. Jean Cox kept her vacation plans as scheduled.

I made arrangements for Jean to stay at the guesthouse for the three days allowed at a time, for single girls. (Married women can stay five days at a time as they don't make so many phone calls.) We went to New York on my (July 4th) three-day pass. See Chapter 6 for details.

I discussed with her Mother, the idea of me marrying Jean and her comment was that Jean was 21 and she had no objections to me. I told her that we would not get married until I got out of the service next Spring.

About this time the Mess Sergeant went to the

Mess/Supply Officer and asked for someone to type up his daily menus as his fingers were very crippled up with arthritis, making typing difficult. So, from then on, I was a Clerk-Typist in the Mess Hall. (As far as I know, it still is not an authorized position in 2021.)

Company P had four Mess Hall buildings and served meals in two of them for the time I was there. Well, one was used for storage of "excess" tables/supplies/equipment. The menus had to be typed up daily and posted at both entrances of the two buildings in use. (I don't remember whether I could use carbon paper or not. Probably had to type each one separately). I also checked the three sample trays (one for each meal) in the refrigerator for "accuracy" relative to the menu. The sample trays were for the Battalion "Mess" officer who could show up at any time and check the status of the Company Mess Hall. The Mess Sergeant would take certain "liberties" with the items on the trays depending on what food was actually available in the kitchen.

Every morning, the Mess Sergeant would send me to the Orderly Room with his request for "detail" soldiers for non-KP duties (clean the grounds/buildings, or whatever). I would then march them back to the Mess Hall. Other than that, I was quite free to roam about the company grounds, unless the Mess Sergeant, Assistant Mess Sergeant, butcher and baker were playing cards on the "balcony" of the barracks behind the Mess Hall where the sergeant's desk was located. I needed to watch for the Battalion inspector, or some other person of importance who came by. I then warned them, so the Sergeant could get down the ladder to his desk and the fellows could cover the card table with an army blanket (inside the barracks). The inspector always checked out the kitchen first (remember the sample trays?). And then went back to the sergeant's desk which was in the back end of the Mess Hall.

When the baker (a Frenchman) was going into town to drink, he fixed a meal of fried bacon, onions, potatoes and eggs to "line his stomach" so as to avoid having a hangover. I have no proof that it worked. However, in the real world, that is often called a farmer's breakfast.

After some time (weeks?), the Mess Sergeant and the butcher managed to get themselves transferred to the "Black Forest" of Germany. Then Staff Sergeant Jerry De Michelle became the Mess Sergeant. He had been the Assistant Mess Sergeant. He would occasionally pick up an egg out of a carton and poke his thumb through the shell and swallow the egg. He said that was to check the freshness of the eggs.

The Mess Halls were expected to have a certain amount of "flatware" (knives, forks and spoons). To keep the count up, Sergeant DeMichele would arrange for a pickup and driver to take us to a nearby Virginia prison farm that routinely picked up the garbage from Fort Belvoir and from restaurants, hotels, etc. in DC. Some flatware got into the garbage when dropped by soldiers as they cleaned the garbage off their mess trays. The prison farm sorted the flatware from the "animal food" and bagged it up for retrieval by those places from which it came. Sorting was not done by individual type, just lumped together by weight. The Fort got a certain amount, as did the other comers. When we got it back to the Fort, we just put it in the unused Mess Hall. No one counted it while I was there.

During that Summer, our Commanding officer's wife died of cancer and was buried in Arlington Cemetery. A few of us attended the burial. I don't recall any details about a funeral.

About that time, Company P got a new Supply/ Mess officer who had been a classmate in TEOCS.

He was a quiet, friendly fellow from nearby Maryland and owned some racehorses. We sometimes walked across the grounds together and he seemed to enjoy "catching" a soldier who wasn't properly dressed (gig line not straight or something) or didn't properly salute him. (The "gig" line was from the neck to the crotch, shirt and trousers in a straight line.)

There was a small detachment of Air Force personnel at Company P to process those Air Force personnel who came to the Fort for certain classes.

A few soldiers assigned to company P were from the Signal Corps. They were responsible for some radio equipment used around the Fort. It was interesting to sit in a room full of Short Wave radios and talk/listen to people from around the world. They also set up the microphones for the USO entertainers. I went along with them one evening when a trio of young ladies came to entertain. (The Bell sisters whose mother traveled with them.) Shows are different when you see them from back stage. What I can remember is that they sang: "The Little White Cloud That Cried." This song was still being recorded in the 21st century.

27 July - The Armistice was signed yesterday! The Korean Conflict is OVER! The third Mess Hall opened and now I have a bit more paper work.

28 July - We had veal cutlets for supper and beef stew the next day.

29 July - A hot day! I worked up a sweat sorting the rations between Mess Halls.

30 July - Got new bunks and mattresses in the barracks today. They look real nice, but too hot to work. I went to the OCS swimming pool and played cards with a Master Sergeant's kids.

7 August - Colonel Browning, Commandant of TEOCS, is going to Omaha, Nebraska to take over the job of District Engineer with that he will get his star and become a Brigadier General. We had 5 in 1 rations today. So, I took home some salt, sugar and ketchup.

8 August - Jean came from Evansville. My "Mess Hall" notes are combined with our apartment living notes (Chapter 7), until she goes back to Evansville at the end of February 1954. Then my "Mess Hall" notes pick up in Chapter 8 (back on Post) and continue until I am in Evansville as a civilian.

CHAPTER 6

New York City and Marriage

Jean Cox came on vacation in July 1953 when I was originally scheduled to graduate from TEOCS (after being set back). Since she had always wanted to go to New York City, we arranged to go there by train over a three-day weekend. A lady at the USO was from Brooklyn and gave us some "pointers" ideas about NYC. We stayed at the Hotel Commodore and had separate rooms, on different floors. (Important in those days.) We saw the play "South Pacific" with most of the original cast. Even the fellow who could roll his stomach and make the ship "tattoo" on it roll with the waves.

On Saturday, we took the Staten Island ferry for five cents each and didn't get off. We had been alerted to stay on and not have to pay another 5-cents each to go back to Manhattan. We walked up Broadway from Battery Park to 82nd Street, going past Wall Street and Trinity Church, which was founded in 1698. (It is an Episcopal church still in use in 2021. It owns several pieces of property around it and is worth a few million dollars.)

Postcard photo from 1950's

We took a bus back to the area of our hotel. Our ankles were black from the street "air."

Along the way, a fellow lounging against a wall said Hello to Jean. He had been stationed at Camp Breckinridge and met her in Evansville. Jean had suggested that it would be interesting to see someone she knew in NYC. I learned later that half of the recruits sent to Breckinridge were from the East Coast and half were from the mid-west.

On Sunday, we walked over the George Washington Bridge to Brooklyn. (For some reason, the Brooklyn Bridge was closed.) We ended up in the factory district and everything was closed. We finally found a small eatery that was open and when seated noticed that we were across the street from a subway entrance. After eating, we took the subway to Chinatown and back to our hotel area.

When we got back to Fort Belvoir, the lady at the USO asked us what we had done and she questioned how we did all that in three days. We told her we walked and she said, "Nobody walks in New York."

Jean and I had corresponded by telephone and mail weekly and had discussed marriage with the thought that we would do that when I got out of the Army the next April. We thought about having the wedding at the Lutheran Church in Evansville, Indiana and then perhaps moving to South Dakota where I would return to farming and use the GI bill to go to college for a degree in Civil Engineering.

The following Tuesday evening, we discussed the question of marriage and agreed to check out the rules/laws in Virginia the next day with the Chaplain. (Jean was scheduled to go back to Evansville, by train, on Friday.)

We met with Chaplain Gomer S. Rees in his office on Wednesday morning and he learned that, in Virginia, the "couple" could get the required blood test done and take it to a doctor for verification and then take it to the Court House and get the marriage license. If you let the info move through the mail, it took three days. So, we got a fellow from Company P to take us around to these places and we arranged for the Chaplain to marry us that evening at 8 or 8:30 PM.

As I recall, there was a $6 charge for a blood test, a $3 office charge at the doctor's office and $4 charge at the court house. We got a new dress and a wedding ring for Jean. She had brought "my" ring along from Evansville. The fellow, who drove us around, took us out for supper. Another couple, named Ed and Lucy Meyer, agreed to be our witnesses. They were also Lutherans (Wisconsin Synod) and Chaplain Rees was a Lutheran.

LEONARD C. MEYER & LOIS JEAN COX MARRIED 22 JUL 53 BY MAJ. GOMER S. REES AT FORT BELVOIR VIRGINIA CHAPEL No. 1

Major Gomer S. Rees, left, new chief chaplain of Berlin Command, and Mrs. Rees are received by Bishop Otto Dibelius at his Berlin home.

It was a drizzly night, from about 4 PM on, and the Chaplain was late. He was entertaining the Japanese Ambassador's daughter at his house and had to miss his dessert to come to Chapel #1 for our wedding. After the service, there were four Lutherans and four Meyers in front of the altar. (In the 1970's we drove to DC with our three children and took them to see Chapel #1)

Afterwards we went to the Phone Exchange to call our folks and tell them what we had done. Jean told her folks and I told mine. Then we switched phones and talked to our new "in-laws." We surprised her Mom and my Dad. Her Dad and my Mom had guessed that we would get married when we got together. (Well, we were 21.)

Jean took the train back to Evansville that Friday and gave Bucyrus-Erie her two-week notice. Then she came back to DC by train.

We needed a car and Jean had some money saved. (I didn't have any.) We bought a '46 Buick, two-tone blue. Cost was $495, plus taxes, title, and license, for a total of $511, without a spare tire. (Neither of us thought to open the trunk.) Hope we don't have problems with it. (Wishful thinking) The salesman was kind enough to find us a spare.

I needed a driver's license in Virginia. (Not required in South Dakota at that time.) The driver's test included a color blindness test. (Now all green traffic signal lights have blue in them, so that test is no longer needed.) When we get some money saved up, we can swap it off for something better, maybe a Ford. We went into DC to get Jean's trunk, which we kept in the car until we got into a larger apartment.

CHAPTER 7

Apartment Living

After a long and tiresome trip (by train) Jean got to DC at midnight, last night (August 8, 1953). A mouse kept crawling around where Jean was sitting and poking his head out. She jumped up the first time she saw it and the woman in front of her thought it was funny that she was afraid of a "little ole' mouse."

While Jean was in Evansville, I rented a shared apartment for $88 a month. The apartment is beautiful: hardwood floors, modern furniture, carpets, pretty painted walls and tile bathroom. The landlady, Mrs. Viola Froneyberger, helped me figure out what to get at the store. I spent $6.04. Eggs cost $0.79 a dozen, and butter $0.89 a pound. Rent control is off and it has gone up $10 a month in the DC vicinity. A new experience, I mowed the landlady's lawn with an electric lawnmower (corded). I had a ride to and from work for $2 a week. The bus would cost at least $3.50 a week.

We went to see "So This Is Love" (Grace Moore's life story) at the theater on Post. Then to the Service Club for a variety show. Two ladies there gave us a cute little folding table. There is no room for it in our apartment.

Two boxes, shipped from Evansville, arrived. We didn't open them, so we didn't know if the dishes got broken or not. We decided to not open them until we get settled somewhere else. There is no room for them here. The landlady is nice and so is the place. But, Jean feels like we are visiting and she wants our own private apartment.

We finally found an apartment in the basement of a house in Alexandria, about five blocks from the George Washington Masonic Memorial. It had a small kitchen, large living/bedroom and a bath. The "landlord" was a couple named Garrett who owned two farms and two houses. He bred Angus cattle. He was a Realtor who was trying to retire from the business. They live in Alexandria during the school year so their 8-year old daughter could go to school. Their other house was near the Blue Ridge Parkway. We stayed there until we moved to Indiana.

The first meal Jean fixed was hamburgers, mashed potatoes and corn. The next night she fixed Salisbury steak (hamburger), mashed potatoes and peas. She experimented with making gravy. She had never made iced tea, but tried that evening. Her coffee was pretty good. She made it in a pan. I don't drink it at all.

13 August 1953 - Meanwhile, back at the Mess Halls, the big (monthly) inspection was conducted and one Mess Hall got a score of 99 and the other got 98. Both the Mess Sergeant, and the Assistant Mess Sergeant got drunk that night.

14 August - We went to the PX and got a few things, a skillet and an iron. With the car, we can get our groceries at the Commissary for less money. We get tickets to several shows in DC from the Service Club. We went to see "High Button Shoes" in Rock Creek Park. The tickets were for $3 seats, perfect, and didn't cost us a cent. Well, we did have to pay a total of $1.98 for round trip bus fare and ride three buses each way. Another evening, we went to DC to see Louis Armstrong. We are getting 18 miles per gallon with car. I had to put in two new gears and a pinion ring in the rear end. It has a rebuilt motor. Now the only noise is a squeaky fan belt.

Jean filed for unemployment (from Indiana) at the local unemployment office. She will get $27 a week. We drove over to Arlington Cemetery, and walked around Lee's Mansion. We went to Mt. Vernon on Sunday afternoon.

Found a private apartment for only $67.50 a month in a nice part of town, about five blocks from the George Washington Masonic Memorial and near a bus stop, and mailbox. The address is 23 Chapman Street, Alexandria, Virginia. It is in a basement with a bath, kitchen and combination living/bedroom. They gave us the key and a few days free rent to clean it up. Jean got "sandpaper" hands from cleaning the kitchen and bathroom floors, on her hands and knees, and cleaning the bath tub, commode and lavatory, stove, refrigerator, cupboards, sink, etc.

Private entrance. The owners are moving back upstairs the 8th of September as they live somewhere else, near the Blue Ridge Parkway, in the summer. Their 8-year old daughter goes to school here. Mrs. Garrett was a schoolteacher and he is retiring from Real Estate. He is also an Angus cattle breeder and has two farms.

18 August - $15 for AAA membership was money well spent as I already had a flat tire. Realized I didn't have a jack. The spare was no good and this tire was not repairable, so it cost me $2.50 for their attempt to fix it. I took it over to the car dealership and got a different spare and AAA put that one on. They didn't have the right size and had to get one from someplace else. (Another day without a spare.)

23 August - Jean got a job at the first place she went. The Service Club suggested the Community Chest. It is temporary, until December 1 and pays $100 every two weeks. (before deductions)

25 August - Back at the Mess Halls, we had to prepare for the annual IG (Inspector General) inspection. They inspect all Army camps both here and overseas. I worked most of the weekend at the Mess Halls, fixed up the Sergeant's desk and the refrigerators and told the detail fellows what to do. There were a lot of excess C-Rations to get rid of, so I took some home.

31 August - The car dealer gave me a spare tire. Then we took the car to a creek on Fort Belvoir, drove in the creek and washed it. Drove on into camp and got a couple of ice cream cones. Stopped at a stop sign. Heard a loud snap when I started up and then the car would not move. Got AAA out again. He tried to pull it forward and the right rear wheel came off, bending the fender skirt and the door slightly. Broken axle! Pulled it backwards to a service station and they were familiar with the car and the previous owner. They said it was OK, except for needing new brakes. So, I had them put on while they had it. Good thing I was getting paid the next day.

By this time, Jean and I had both experienced homesickness. Both enjoyed our radio. Seemed like every Saturday something happened to the car and we had to stay home all weekend. With the car, we can get groceries at the Commissary. A pound of Maxwell House coffee was $0.87 and it was $1.05 in town. Now I have five tires on the car. Jean bought one and we charged one. I had a rider, to and from, camp. That will help with expenses.

We had a cook from South Dakota who was a Sergeant. One day he asked me to take a chicken to his place of residence (a mobile home) and another time he asked me to take a pound of butter. (You can see how naive I was.) Before I got in real trouble, I was warned not to do that any more, as he was being watched and would not be with us much longer. Sure enough he was gone shortly after that. I never learned what happened to him, or his family.

On Sunday mornings I would drive to the nearby drugstore and get a Sunday paper. One Sunday an 8-year old girl, on a bicycle, came out from between two cars and I bumped her over. She was taken to the hospital and checked out with no physical injury. I went to her home later and talked to her folks. They seemed pleased that I did that. Later, my insurance agent scolded me for "getting involved."

10 September - We had the Quartermaster inspection today. They inspect all mattresses.

14 September - Got a Fort Myer hospital card for Jean, in case she needs it. Learned that she will have to go to the Fort Myer hospital as we live on the North side of King Street in Alexandria. One Sunday we drove up to Fort Myer to locate the hospital. Jean asked to try driving the car, thinking that we were on the edge of DC and would soon be in the country. That was not to be and she soon stopped and let me drive again. She took Drivers' Education while in High School, but refused to take the Driver's Test.

One Saturday evening we drove around DC through Fort McNair, past Walter Reed Hospital and on Ohio Drive to Hains Point. We stopped, like in courting days, and watched the moon go down over Maryland. Then, lunch at the Hot Shoppe and home.

Jean really likes her job. She is kinda proud of herself, as she is the only real typist in the office. The other two are more like me, "hunt and peck". Anyway she can type a lot faster than the 45 words per minute required in Virginia. Indiana requires 60 words per minute.

3 October - I gave a speech on Mess Management to the Company Cadre. I made PFC (Private First Class) and get $14 more per month. The car needed a new clutch, another $53.55.

Jean began having "morning sickness" about the first of October. Our first appointment was at Fort Myer on October 27th. Our guess is that she is a month and half along. I am learning a lot I never knew about childbirth and people. One night, Jean dreamt she had twin girls. If it is a boy, we will name it Michael Jay. (After a few years and two girls, we got our boy.)

One Saturday we went into DC to the U.S.O. Club and then did some window-shopping. Too expensive to go to a show in DC as they cost from $1.00 to $1.50 and the same shows are only $.25 at the Fort and usually shown there before they are in DC. A neighbor in Alexandria had a TV and invited us over to watch "The Life of Riley."

Jean was home from work for four days (morning sickness). I stayed home with her as needed, with the approval of my Mess Sergeant. Jean's "bosses" like her so well that they are going to pay her for the four days she was in bed.

14 October - Mess Halls are being fixed up with new gas ranges in the kitchens and new refrigerators.

They have to put new pillars underneath the floors and more concrete on the floors.

One evening we "sat" with Mary Sue, the little eight-year old girl who lives upstairs. Her Father had gone on a 600-mile trip to Tennessee, and her mother was at a PTA meeting. The girl has a pony and a dog on their 800-acre farm. Her mother, Mrs. Garrett, came home about 9:30 PM and we visited until almost midnight. They had been to the West Coast and back and stayed one night in Mitchell, South Dakota. Since that is about 50 miles from my home, there was a lot of visiting.

We went on about a 200-mile trip to the Blue

Ridge Skyline Drive one Sunday. This was a bit too much for Jean in her condition. We went to see the Doctor in Fort Myer. He gave Jean four different kinds of pills: Sulfate, Vitamins, Calcium and Phosphate. She got a complete checkup and a shot for the vomiting. Go back on Saturday, and three times next week. That's all of the shots. Then back on November 24 for monthly checkup. (Homesick on the side.) She is a scared girl. She had pyelitis when she was little and was told then that she would have a time when she had a baby. That has concerned her all her life. I convinced her that the good Lord would keep her well for me and help us through. That seemed to help her. Doctor gave us a book on Prenatal Care, put out by Pet Milk Co. (A good book without advertisements.) Doctor set the birth date as May 4. (Karen Kay Meyer was born at Deaconess Hospital, Evansville, Indiana on May 2, 1954.)

3 November - While in Company P, I went to the dental clinic and got a bridge in place of the one tooth partial that I had since the summer of '52. I learned that the dentist (a Captain) had a practice on Park Avenue in New York City. He wasn't busy and I had time to make several trips over to him, so he made the bridge himself. His dental assistant was a German lady and she checked the needles before letting him use them. She would drag the needle across the palm of her hand to verify that it had no barbs. One did, so I was glad she did that.

That procedure would not be allowed today. The dentist ground off the back of one anchor tooth and made a piece for it and then he did the other anchor tooth and finally he made the new tooth to fit between the two anchor teeth. That was in early 1954. That bridge lasted over 50 years. I had it replaced at the Indiana University Dental School with a three-tooth bridge as one of the "anchor" teeth was cracked when I lost a tooth in Camp Breckinridge, in '52. It came apart when the student removed the one tooth bridge.

Because of Jean's being sick and missing work, I took her keys down to her office and told them she was quitting. They wouldn't let her quit. They said it was too hard to find someone as "intelligent and quick to catch on" as Jean. They would rather have her for one day a week than some others for five.

The shots helped. Jean usually feels good, if I get up and fix her breakfast, one fried egg, two pieces of bacon, one cup of coffee, one piece of toast and orange juice. I sometimes have an egg and bacon with her. Then I can eat, too, before I go to work. Of course, it would be cheaper to wait until I get to camp and eat a couple boxes of cereal and some sandwiches.

I have been having some attacks of appendicitis. I told Dad that I have no plans for returning to the farm, as Jean would not live there.

10 November - (Sunday) I had Guard Duty all day. It was inside, at the head of a stairs, directly in front of the front door.

Mrs. Garrett invited Jean to go to church with her and her twin sister. Her sister is a schoolteacher and Mrs. Garrett was before she got married. They went to Christ Episcopal Church, Alexandria, where George Washington worshiped. Jean got to see Washington's pew. The inside of the church is all painted white and looks pretty.

We had a five-inch snow early in November. I enjoyed driving in it. I had the car inspected on Armistice Day as required in Virginia. I had to have new king pins put in for $18.75. The inspection sticker cost 50 cents.

Jean's folks came for a visit. Her Dad had his foot broken at work and it was in a cast. He managed to drive OK. Jean's Dad wasn't feeling too good when they got here. He took a nap and then felt better. I was supposed to take a PT test one morning but, it was raining and I had my work done, so Sergeant Roberts told me to go home and be with my mother-in-law. I took my in-laws to DC for a quick look around. Their visit was too short. They brought some food made in Indiana. While here, Mrs. Garrett took Jean and her mother out for dinner one day and was down to visit nearly every day. She told Jean's mother that she was

Jean's mother away from home.

Mrs. Ryan, the lady who gave Jean her job said the same thing. So, Jean has been pretty well cared for.

The Coxes left for home early on the Friday before Thanksgiving and were home by 3 PM on Saturday.

We made plans to go out to the camp for Thanksgiving Dinner for $1.20 each.

Company P
9829th TSU-CE TECR
Fort Belvoir, Virginia

THANKSGIVING MENU

Shrimp Cocktail with Sauce and Lemon Wedges

Assorted Relishes

Roast Turkey with Sage Dressing and Giblet Gravy

Cranberry Sauce

Mashed Potatoes   Candied Sweet Potatoes

Buttered Peas   Corn O'Brien

Waldorf Salad

Parkerhouse Rolls   Butter

Pumpkin Pie with Whipped Cream

Fruit Cake

Assorted Fresh Fruits   Assorted Candy

Mixed Nuts

Coffee

We went out to camp on a Friday night and heard Geoffrey O'Hara, the man who composed "K-K-K-Katy," "I Walked Today Where Jesus Walked" and "There Is No Death," and other songs. Saturday night we went into DC and saw "Martin Luther." It cost $2.40 total.

Month of December - The newly equipped Mess Hall kitchen was busy with Christmas parties for the officers and their families.

L to R: MSG De Michele, Mess Steward; Stufflebean, Ass't. Steward; Hugh Ivester, Cook (Gastonia NC); Massey, Cook; Erskine, Cook; Lowing, Cook; Joseph Allen, Cook, (CA) Di Pinto Cook, SGT Arlis Stacey, Cook; (Ohio); COL Blooms, Reg't. CDR; CPL Ponook, Cook (MD); Mr. Sam Shepherd, Reg't. Food Adv.

L to R: PFC Louis Di Pinto (Chicago); 1LT William F. Sweeny, CDR Co. P; PV2 John Lowing (Gastonia N.C.); SSG Clyde Stufflebean (Ft. Worth, TX); MSG Jerry D. DeMichele (N.Y.); PV2 Jerry Massey (Gulfport MS); CPL Wallace Erskine (LA CA); CPL Parks (MO).

12 December - I passed the PT test OK and now have sore muscles. Donated another pint of blood. That makes 6 pints, 3/4 gallon. I have had several attacks of appendicitis. As long as they are only pains in the side that go away with ice packs, there is no urgency about surgery.

Jean has been riding to work with a Mr. Levinson, one of the brothers who owns the Levinson clothing store, near where she works. He picks up the people waiting for the bus when he comes by. The first day she wore her new maternity dress, the skirt fell to her ankles when she got out of his car. She was embarrassed. One of the women riders held her things while she picked up her skirt and tied it in a knot. She had only used a bow-knot earlier.

That evening, we went to see "Give a Girl a Break" with Marge and Gower Champion, and Debbie Reynolds.

20 December - We went to see the children's Christmas program at Christ Church one evening because the little girl upstairs, Mary Sue, was in it. The Garretts gave us some Virginia Homemade Pork Sausage. It is ground and mixed by a Packing House, as homemade as you can get here. They put a lot of lard in theirs. I bought a pound box of Whitman's Sampler at the PX for $1.60, regular price is $2.25 and the Commissary price is $1.35. Interesting.

I cut down a small cedar tree out in the thick woods (technically, I stole it) with a dull hatchet. Well, Mrs. Garrett liked it, so I got one for her. (She didn't like the one Mr. Garrett had brought home for her.)

24 December - Jean thought she was getting over the (morning) sickness, because we went out for dinner Christmas Eve and she had a full course lobster dinner. It consisted of shrimp cocktail, clam chowder, and five oysters on the half shell. Then, came the lobster, stuffed with dressing, dill pickle, tossed salad, French fries, corn, biscuits, iced tea and chocolate ice cream cake. She ate until she thought she would be sick, nearly two hours. She said that she could probably finish the lobster if she had another hour. After about an hour of rest at home, we went to a drug store and I called my folks. Jean said she was hungry and had a chocolate soda while I talked to my folks. Then we went to the Candlelight Service at the Lutheran church. We then came home and unwrapped presents. I got Jean a metal ironing board. (Still have it in 2021.)

25 December - Christmas day we went up to Garretts for a big turkey dinner. It was a wonderful Christmas. In this part of the country, everyone starts calling on friends/neighbors Christmas Eve and keep it up for about four days afterward. Each house serves drinks. So when we first went upstairs, the neighbors were there. They were serving eggnog that they buy from the milkman. Not enough liquor to taste. There was a millionaire among the guests (we learned later that he is Mrs. Garrett's brother). Nothing made Jean sick.

However, the next day we went for a ride and may have ridden too far as she was sick.

The following day Jean was eating a bit again, tomato soup, half a glass of milk, two crackers, one pear and a couple of potato chips, strung out over two hours. It stayed down. After Jean's bath, we went upstairs to sit with Mary Sue for a while. The Garretts really like us and want us to stay here as long as possible.

27 December - I took our laundry to the Fort Belvoir Laundry weekly. Once, after picking up the laundry, I put it in the back seat and started out of the parking lot. The laundry bag rolled off the seat and, instead of stopping, I turned around to put it back on the seat and ran into a utility pole, knocking out the left front headlight and twisting the frame a little. It took $35 to fix the frame plus the cost of a new headlight. So, we didn't go out New Year's Eve. Instead, we went upstairs and stayed with Mary Sue and watched the ball come down on TV. December 31 was Jean's last day to work for the Community Chest.

10 January 1954 - We plan to have Jean fly home

and then I will follow by car, after I get out. I'm going to try selling Wearever (Aluminum Cookware). It is a good racket and I can do it part time.

13 January - Over five-inches of snow fell this morning. There was so much traffic it took me an hour and a half to get to work. It was cold too. Then, I went home at noon and changed clothes to walk guard duty. Kids are out of school. Mary Sue got the mail for Jean. She was allowed outside two minutes at a time.

16 January - I tried 40 homes and couldn't get anyone interested in the free gift from Wearever. Jean had left the tub water running and went out to empty the wastebasket. She locked herself out. She had just washed her head and only had on a sweater (over her dress) and no socks in the snow. The Garrett's were not home. She went four houses down the street after help. She found a couple of men there who came over and tried all the windows and were trying to pick the lock with a knife and bobby pin. Then, I got home and the tub had not run over.

19 January - I have displayed my Wearever set once. NO sale.

21 January - I made a $119 sale (made a $22 commission). That broken headlight and damaged fender cost me $104. I had to borrow money for my demonstration set: A small ($16.65) sale. $5.00

for me.

23 January - (Jean's 22nd Birthday). Another five-inches of snow fell and having traffic delays from the earlier snow, I decided to take the back road into the Fort. Well, "the best laid plans of mice and men oft go awry." I got stuck out in the middle of nowhere. I walked back to a house with lights on and knocked on the door. The elderly lady was very gracious and called AAA for me as well as my boss at the Mess Hall. Then I waited...and waited for the AAA truck. While waiting, I watched the lady's small (maybe 10-inch) TV on top of her old radio console. This was my first experience with daytime TV. Needless to say, I was probably later than if I would have taken the highway.

26 January - Back to camp at 6:15 PM for a CBR (Chemical, Biological and Radiological) class. Then headed to an 8 PM appointment in Alexandria. Took Jean to Doc again today. Everything was going OK. She weighed 109 (gained three pounds per month.) I made $26 last week selling Wearever. I had only one showing this week. I took Jean a pretty and delicious birthday cake.

5 February - Jean worked one day at the Community Chest as one lady was with her husband who was having surgery.

10 February - We planned to send Jean to Evansville, by plane, the end of February. Eastern

Airlines was the only direct plane to Evansville. She will leave at 8 PM, Sunday evening, February 28th, and be in Evansville at 10:06 PM. We will ship her clothes by freight and store everything else in Garrett's basement until I go with the car in April.

My sister, Wanda, was in DC on a Farmers Union tour. I picked her, and two girl friends, up on Sunday about 4 PM. I surprised them in the lobby of the Dodge Hotel and showed them Fort Belvoir and took in a movie "Walking My Baby Back Home" with Donald O'Connor and Janet Leigh. Dad had sent some money so we five could go to a movie.

On Monday, the last stop on their tour was the George Washington Masonic Memorial, about five blocks from our apartment. I joined them for the tour and then brought them to our place for supper that Jean had fixed. After supper, we took them to DC and went to the Farmers Union meeting at the Dodge Hotel. They sang some country songs and then had two long-winded speakers. Jean said that was her first and LAST Farmers Union meeting.

12 February - Wanda left this morning, so we went in last night and told her goodbye. Jean was going up to stay with Mary Sue the next day so she invited Mrs. Garrett and Mary Sue down for supper that night.

Valentine's Day Celebration - The Mess Hall kitchen was busy again providing a special heart cake for everyone to enjoy.

L to R: MSG Jerry D. DeMichele (NY); PFC William Metlharm (Decatar, IL); CPL Donald Alpereta (Pittsburgh, PA); PV2 Lewis Allen (PA); SGT Pedro "Poncho" Salazar (TX); SGT Willie Wilson (SC); PFC Leonard C. Meyer (me).

18 February - I have everything packed for shipment to Evansville. Sunday and Tuesday we went sightseeing. We were able to visit: Sunday- Capitol, Botanical Gardens, Library of Congress; Tuesday- Bureau of Engraving and Printing, White House, F.B.I., National Art Gallery, Supreme Court and Ford Theater. I had a slight misfortune last night. I broke the clutch rod on the car. Cost $4 to repair rod and eye bolt that adjusts the spring. Jean fixed dinner for the Garretts (and us): Fried chicken, mashed potatoes, gravy, peas, corn, combination salad, hot rolls, peaches and whipped cream with a bought angel food cake and coffee. On Tuesday we went to Fort Myer. We didn't see Jean's regular doctor; but did get her chart to take to Evansville.

20 February - I sent the freight items this Saturday morning. They should be delivered to Ronald and Gladys Cox's door either Tuesday or Wednesday. There may be a $5 or $6 charge on them. We will pay Ronald and Gladys Cox when we get there. I got $50.00 partial pay for Jean to fly home. We live close to the airport; so, Jean took the bus to the airport and had about an hours visit with Barbara Windels (a neighbor from Evansville).

23 February - I was off work yesterday for George Washington's Birthday. They have quite a celebration here in Alexandria. We got to see the big parade. It is a 30-year tradition to have ridiculous sales. TV sets and radios for $0.99. Also, a '40 Ford for $0.99. The fellow who got it went there at 6:30 AM Sunday morning to be first in line at 9:00 AM Monday morning. People went with blankets and food to get in line early.

CHAPTER 8

Back on Post

1 March 1954 - I have moved back on post as Jean flew to Evansville, in a four-engine Constellation flown by Eastern Airlines. The Doctor suggested that she fly rather than go over the mountains by car. Remember, the baby is due May 4th. There was a shooting in the House of Representatives. A woman from Puerto Rico shot at least one Representative, put a hole in the ceiling (I saw that later) and messed up at least one desk. A reporter from radio station WRC caught her. My bad tire went flat and I had to get a different one ($18). I made a Wearever sale and got $10.05. I went to the Service Club and watched the dancers.

2 March - The First Sergeant wanted me out of the Mess Hall since that is the Mess Steward's job and we have three Army ones and three Air Force ones. Well, the Mess Sergeant wouldn't stand for that, so finally the First Sergeant gave in. I am giving up the Wearever business. I am not a salesman at all. Considering that we have a set, I didn't lose any money. Frankly, I'm a little scared about going to work in the city. I plan to go at it as I did the Army. Get the most out of it for me and laugh it off when things don't go so well.

3 March - I went to Ash Wednesday service and saw the WAC who works in Food Service and the one who runs X-ray in Dental Clinic # 1. She had four friends with her. We, Milhorn and I, gave them a ride from Chapel #2 to Service Club # 1 cafeteria. They had a cup of coffee and I had tea. We visited a while. The Thrift Shop sold my "officer's brass" and I got $3.20 (paid $11).

I had "training" this PM.

1st hour - Dismounted drill. Got mixed up and took the GI bus over to the Essayons Playhouse and back. Then, I played Shuffleboard.

2nd hour - Character Guidance - Essayons Playhouse. Good homes are essential to Democracy and women are essential to homes (the Jewish Chaplain said that is why the Army has WACS.) Ha!

3rd hour - T.I. and E. A good discussion on our Economic System, Co-ops, Monopolies, Trusts and Labor Unions.

4th hour – Inspection

I went back to the barracks. There will be a surprise clothing inspection some evening next week by the CO. So, I had to mark my clothes. I backed into a tree and knocked out the light over the rear license plate. Sunday night an MP stopped me and told me that my right front parking light was out. I took the car on Saturday and got them fixed.

4 March - Last night the exhaust pipe came off the water heater and the barracks filled with smoke. I was up at 6 AM this morning.

7 March - I drove around DC and looked at some of the sights, I am the guide. Yesterday we went through the submarine and the Park and the Zoo. The boys are pretty good about putting gas in the tank. I helped two girls change a tire.

10 March - Travel pay from Fort Belvoir to Sioux Falls is 6 cents a mile for 1244 miles, $100 mustering out pay, about $130 for leave time not used and another $100 in May also mustering out pay. Total is about $405.84. We had our biggest inspection of the year in the Mess Hall today. Sure glad that is over. Passed it with flying colors. Nothing wrong.

11 March - The Sauter-Finegan Orchestra, (American swing jazz orchestra) was very good. First show had a small crowd, but the 8 PM one had a long line waiting. Some of the boys fixed my bed while I was out this evening. They piled four mattresses, one bed, one wall locker and my footlocker on top of it. Guess they had fun doing it! Oh well, boys will be boys 'til they grow up. Started training my replacement, a cook who is a Corporal.

13 March - I sent a St. Patrick's Day card to an OLD Irish friend of mine at home. (She was Dad's third grade teacher.)

14 March - I went to the USO dance last night at the Jewish Community Center. I had a lot of fun. It was all decorated for St. Patrick's Day. After the dance, we went to Gusti's — a real Italian place. I had veal Parmesan (veal with a kind of cheese sauce over it. Spaghetti was served on the side.) Very good. Had two Italians with me and they both liked the food.

15 March - I went to theater #3 last night and saw "The Command" in Cinemascope. A very good picture. I sat with two WACs on one side and two WACs on the other side. I ate popcorn out of two different bags. Shirley (the X-ray girl) was one of the four. I took them back to their barracks. One changed into her uniform and then I took her to the hospital where she works.

17 March - I received a Commendation letter from Lieutenant Sweeny today. It is a form letter given to all dischargees upon completion of their tour of service. Of course, civilians don't know that and one can use it as a letter of recommendation or character reference. Saturday we have another inspection. This time a standby, with foot and wall lockers open. Nothing too good for a soldier like me! Ha! I have driven 1040 miles since Jean went back to Evansville. I filled the gas tank three times.

17 March - (Second letter) I went to see "Ma

and Pa Kettle at Home" and then to a square dance last night. I went into DC yesterday and toured the Folger's Shakespearean Library. Canceled my Wearever contract. Got a pass and went to see the House of Representatives in action.

18 March - Another fellow from P Company and I went over to the Essayons Playhouse and listened to a Separation Orientation from 1:30 PM to about 2:45 PM. I learned a few things. I talked to the fellow who works the Red Cross Blood Mobile about me giving blood for Jean's use, if necessary. The Blood Center in Washington, DC will write to the hospital in Evansville and tell them to draw blood from the Louisville Blood Center. He said that we could use as much blood as is needed.

A veteran has a lot of benefits. I will explain when I get home. The Red Cross fellow said Evansville is the best city to find a job in. He had been to Camp Breckinridge a couple of times.

19 March - I saw the Hollywood Stage show last night, from back stage. The best place to see a stage show. I was with the Signal Corps photographer. He took several pictures in the dressing rooms. One of the girls had a part in "How to Marry a Millionaire." The Bell sisters were there with their mother. They are the ones who sang "The Little White Cloud That Cried, " a while back. I got in free to the movie: "Ride Vaquero" with Howard Keel and Ava Gardner.

Pretty good show. Afterwards, I rode along with the photographer and a couple of his friends to where he had shot the picture they used for display.

Then to a second club and saw their second show at 12:45 AM. A couple of singers and a stripper.

I am checking on the Army paying for bringing the baby into this world. I did a bit of carpentry for the Service Center this afternoon.

21 March - Four hours of training this morning, including inspection. He didn't even check mine. He (the CO) did ask how Jean was and when the baby is due. I told him Jean is fine and baby is due in May. Rained "cats and dogs" Friday night. So, a couple of boys and I took three girls home to Alexandria. They lived near where Mom and Pop stayed when they were here in November. They had to be home by 11:00 PM and it was already 10:45 PM. Of course they were a little late, 11:15 PM. They would have been a lot later and wetter if they had waited for the bus. On the way back to camp, I ran out of gas again and had to call AAA. Yesterday, I went into DC three times, all paying trips. Drove over 200 miles, boy was I tired. I went to church on South Post this morning and met a fellow from the west side of Evansville. Chaplain's hour Saturday AM was on "Prejudice", and was given by the colored Captain, who had coffee in our Mess Hall last month.

23 March - I will have over $300 when I come home. Now that I have been relieved from duty, I just loaf all day. I am going over to South Post and see "Overland Pacific" and then to the square dance at Service Club #1. I have a fellow from Evansville who plans to come with me and has driven the route in twelve hours by himself.

25 March - I have made it today. Corporal, that is! 20 days to go. I have to take charge of a busload of Casuals going to Fort Myer to watch Company P play in the MDW Tournament; my first job as an NCO (Non-commissioned officer). Cherry trees are blooming. Boy, they are beautiful.

27 March - I learned that the Army would not pay for the baby's birth. Sergeant Porter has me scheduled on guard duty next weekend (twenty-four hours), my last weekend here. I'm going to see if I can pull it during the week instead. As a Corporal in the Reserves, I'll get $4.33 for every meeting I attend.

28 March - I saw "Rhapsody" starring Elizabeth Taylor. You must see it. I went to church and had Communion this morning on South Post. Six of us went sightseeing this afternoon. We walked up the Washington Monument. Then, we saw some girls and stopped to talk to them back of the Capitol, near Grant's Monument. There were six of them and six of us. I helped a couple of them change the film in their camera. Then we left and went up North to see the Soldiers Home, and the Franciscan Monastery.

30 March - Yesterday afternoon one of the boys (night baker) and I drove down to Quantico (the Marine base) and looked around for about two hours. Last night, three of us went into DC where Shorty has his dancing lessons, 4 to 6 PM. He is going overseas. While he was there, I went to the National Geographic Society Building and looked at it and the small but interesting museum. Tonight, we went to the square dance and then to Alexandria for coffee (I had tea). I met a nice girl tonight who is a wonderful square dancer. I had a nice visit with her mother who came with her. She wouldn't come out on the A.B. and W. Bus by herself or with girls who pick up a date or dance all night with the same partner. Her boyfriend has just joined the Army, three weeks ago and is in Fort Jackson, South Carolina. I turned in my field jacket and overcoat today and drew a few sets of stripes. Also, I got my two ribbons (Good Conduct and Service).

31 March - I cleared Post yesterday so now all I have to do is turn in my bedding, get my physical, my pay and a farewell lecture and "Bye-Bye" to Belvoir. Then, it's "Back Home Again in Indiana." I was on guard duty tonight rather than Saturday. I had the inside post by the Signal Office, same as in November.

1 April - *Morning* I am still on guard duty and am visiting with the telephone operator. She is originally from South Dakota. Then she moved to Minnesota, and now four years in Virginia. I donated my 8th unit of blood today. Then, I took Shorty into DC again (and a couple other riders) and I went to the National Archives this afternoon. Interesting, they have every state's flag and some historical documents and pictures. I joined the NCO Club yesterday, mostly to keep in good with Sergeant Porter. I went over and played Bingo, grand prize was $100. I didn't win.

2 April - I had quite an evening yesterday, the generator quit. New one was $18.75. Then, changed the oil, $2+. I then drained the radiator, and added a bottle of water pump lubricant to the radiator. So, I am nearly fixed up again. I went down to the submarine again. I don't get paid until the morning of the 14th, so I won't get a very early start.

3 April - I am on my way to Hackensack, New Jersey.

5 April - I had an exciting weekend. Hackensack is between Newark and New York City. I saw the Empire State Building again, from a distance of course. It took about five hours to go up and seven to come back, more traffic. We drove the full length of the New Jersey Turnpike. A swell road. I drove Shorty up there with his clothes. He is leaving Wednesday for 30 days before he goes to Europe. He paid all expenses.

6 April - I cleaned company Supply this morning. I am going to get a canteen and cover, an old style overcoat (horse blanket) and one GI blanket. It's all legal and no expense to me. I went to the NCO Club last night just to see what it was like. I saw DeMichele and met his wife. Boy, she is a beautiful blonde.

7 April - I reminded Jean that I was driving the car to Indiana and that I would find a job, even if I had to drive out into the country and find farm work. Also, I would have about $300 with me and another $200 coming in May. I urged her to trust God to take care of us.

8 April - I have a free ticket to the Exhibition game in Griffith Stadium between the Senators and the Dodgers. A couple of fellows are going, Massey and Lawing and his wife. They are putting in the gas. I went over and visited with Mrs. "T" today. That helped a little, at least someone I can discuss things with. We had wieners and sauerkraut for supper. Oh Boy! "C rations" tomorrow.

9 April - I had my physical today. I am on my way OUT! Also, I had the interview that I am supposed to have next Monday. Now I am free until 10:00

Tuesday. Then, a few records to sign. Wednesday I get paid and then on my way. No more letters from me as a soldier. I went to the square dance to say good-bye to those folks. I haven't heard any more from the fellow who was going to go with me to Evansville.

The fellow at Separation said he had never seen such a high Officer Candidate Test score for anyone with only a High School education. My score was 140. Of the thousands of scores he has seen, he has only seen one higher (155) and that fellow had a Master's degree from College.

10 April - I got up at 9:30. The Supply Sergeant was going to DC along with three other fellows, So, I said for a buck a piece, I'll take you in. That way they caught their 11 AM train and I got a tank of gas. Then I went to QM and got my laundry. Dressed up, blue trousers, white shirt and blue tie. Then Massey and I picked up the Laings and went to Rock Creek Park, and Zoo; then on to the Archives and Art Gallery. We went to the Botanical Gardens. They were closed (Saturday) so we went to the Capitol and got through it before it closed; then to the Lincoln Memorial and to the Hot Shoppe for a light lunch. To Shubert's Theater and saw "Twin Beds." A good show; but not nearly as good as "Guys and Dolls." Boy am I tired. Tomorrow, we are going to Gunston Hall, Woodlawn Mansion,

Mt. Vernon, eat a picnic lunch, and then on to Arlington Cemetery, Lee's Mansion, Tomb of the Unknown Soldier and Masonic Memorial.

12 April - I went over to South Post today and said "Goodbye" to the food service people and Corporal Shirley Smith (Dental Clinic #1). I got our radio at the PX office and the mixer may be here before Wednesday morning. I stopped at Red Cross office and got my gold (blood drop) pin and gallon club certificate. The director here knows a fellow in Evansville. He told me to look that fellow up when I get there. I said "Goodbye" to Mrs. "T" and Miss Betts today. They are both off tomorrow. I plan to call Mrs. Garrett tonight and go there tomorrow night. I will get my uniform ready tonight and pack a few more things. I have to sign records tomorrow morning.

16 April - I got to Evansville at 5:30 AM yesterday. I drove straight through. Left Arlington, Virginia at 11:45 AM on the 14th. Got $427.80 as my last pay. ($81 + for travel pay.) Today, I got my Indiana car license and applied for my driver's license. I joined the Active Reserves and I will go to my first meeting next Tuesday. Since I just got out, I won't have to go to summer camp this year. I will draw $4.33 for each meeting and will get it by check at the end of the month. I have applied for my Social Security card and recorded my Separation papers. I had photo stats made before I left Fort Belvoir. We will go to the Easter Sunrise service at a drive-in. They are showing part of "Prince of Peace" movie. Sure is nice to be home with Jean again.

MISCELLANEOUS INFO:

While again living on post, I would take fellows on tours of DC, provided they filled the gas tank on my car. I often had a car full. Some had been on post for months and hadn't even taken the bus to DC. (Cost less than 50 cents each way.) More than once, we ran out of gas and coasted down a hill into a gas station (on the left side of the highway).

The speed limit on the Shirley Highway decreased about 10 miles per hour, every mile, or so, as one approached DC. I got a total of three speeding tickets in the month and a half I was back on post. Fortunately, my third one was in a different county than the other two. It was only a few days before I left for Evansville. No computers in those days! Three tickets and you had to give up your driver's license.

April - A few days after I got to Evansville, I got a forwarded letter from the Virginia Bureau of Motor Vehicles, or whatever it was called then, telling me to send in my driver's license. By this time I had gotten a driver's license in Indiana, so I sent the Virginia license back to Virginia.

BIOGRAPHY

Leonard C. Meyer

Leonard grew up on a small farm in southeastern South Dakota. He went to grade school in a one-room school two miles from home. His father farmed with horses, as did many neighbors. Leonard learned manual farm work at a very young age.

His father became physically unable to do manual labor when Leonard was a freshman in Humboldt High School. This resulted in Leonard becoming the farmer. Soon his father bought a used Model B John Deere tractor.

Two years after Leonard's graduation from High School he received his draft notice to report for active duty with the U.S. Army. After two years of active duty and the Korean Conflict stopped, Leonard was "separated" from active duty.

By this time, he had married and moved to Evansville, Indiana, where he went to work at the U.S. Post Office. Soon he started attending Evansville College, using the GI bill. He obtained a degree in Mechanical Engineering. After a few months working for the U.S. Air Force in Ohio, Leonard found employment at the Naval Avionics Facility in Indianapolis, Indiana.

He and his wife Jean raised their three children, Karen, Debbie and Mike there and cared for Jean's mother twenty-five years during that time.

Leonard retired from Federal Employment in 1987. He and Jean traveled extensively to all fifty states and over twenty foreign countries. Jean died in 2019 (after 66+ years of marriage) and Leonard is now living alone in their "condo" type home in Greenfield, Indiana.

CPSIA information can be obtained
at www.ICGtesting.com
Printed in the USA
BVHW031230070722
641567BV00013B/1045

9 781937 912628